Stained Glass Tours
Around
Norfolk Churches

By David J. King B.A.

PUBLISHED BY THE NORFOLK SOCIETY
1974

Preface

This book was written at the invitation of the Norfolk Society's Committee for Country Churches. It is intended as one of a series of books on different aspects of our Norfolk churches, designed to follow up their initial publication 'Norfolk Country Churches and the Future', and to continue the encouragement of interest in and concern for our wonderful but threatened heritage of country churches.

The author's main occupation is the preparation of a large, illustrated reference book on all the medieval glass in Norfolk, as part of the international series, *Corpus Vitrearum Medii Aevi*. This is being done under the direction of the British Committee of the C.V.M.A., which is financed by the British Academy. These institutions are in no way directly responsible for this present publication, but many thanks are due to them for the active encouragement which they afford to the study of medieval glass in East Anglia and in many other parts of England, without which this book would not have been written.

Thanks are also due to several other persons and institutions. The School of Fine Arts and Music of the University of East Anglia has provided excellent photographic facilities; the Centre of East Anglian Studies there, in the person of Mrs. Anita Schweinberger, has helped with preparation of the typescript, as has also my wife. My uncle, Mr. Dennis King, provided some of the negatives for the plates and also much other assistance. Mrs. Hilda Strickland gave me new and important information about the work of her father, Ernest Heasman. Mr. Richard Fawcett, Mr. Nigel Morgan and Mr. Richard Marks have all helped with advice and discussion, and the encouragement and enthusiasm of Lady Harrod have been invaluable. Mr. John Piper is to be thanked especially for his generous gift of a cover design. Finally, much gratitude is due to all those incumbents and church wardens who have given the author access and facilities for the study of the glass in their churches.

Contents

Places in the text in **bold type** have a complete entry to themselves.

Introduction

The aim of this little book is simple: to encourage people to visit Norfolk churches and look at the stained glass in them, by providing a series of suggested itineraries with notes on the glass in each of the churches concerned. What is not intended is a comprehensive survey of all the glass in the county, nor a complete description in all aspects of the glass in the churches to be visited. The notes vary in character: some are more descriptive, some give the historical background to the glass and some relate it to other works of art. The underlying principle is to deal with what is particularly interesting in each place and also to give as much essential information as is necessary to understand the context of what is seen. Three types of glass are described: first, and by far the largest group, is the indigenous medieval glass of the 13th to 16th century; second, foreign glass of the 15th and 16th centuries, imported into England from the continent in the 19th century, including several panels which have recently been identified as coming from the cloister glazing of c. 1522-57 of the German monastery at Steinfeld; much more of which has been in the Victoria and Albert Museum, London, since 1928; third, a few examples of the many fine, more modern windows to be found in this county.

Of the medieval glass in Norfolk, there is very little of the 13th century and only a few significant collections of 14th century glass. Christopher Woodforde has briefly summarised the glass of this period and several of the places mentioned by him, along with a few others, appear in the itineraries. As he says, on the whole this glass resembles in quality and design that of contemporary English glass in other parts of the country, but there are a number of cases where the glass does reflect the style of the celebrated group of East Anglian manuscripts of the early 14th century. A figure of St. Barnabas in Downham Market church, for example, is clearly linked to a psalter of c. 1300 made for Ramsey Abbey, in whose patronage this church was at that time.

A complete picture of the 15th century glass of Norfolk has never been given, mainly because of the difficulty of putting the surviving remains into any sort of chronological order. In the period 1400-40, only a few, but important, examples remain. Some of the glass at Saxlingham Nethergate is datable to c. 1400 and fragments at Salle and Litcham are c. 1411-12. The style of the large panels at North Tuddenham and of some of the pieces at Cawston suggests that they were made c. 1420-30 and the next decade probably saw the painting of the glass at Narborough, Ketteringham and West Rudham. The period 1440-50 was that of two highly important series of panels: the magnificent chancel glazing at Salle, whose style seems perhaps to preclude a local origin, and the Infancy Cycle at St. Peter Mancroft, Norwich, which establishes a distinctive Norwich-based style, which continues and develops right up to the end of the century and is seen in various sub-groupings in much of the 15th century glass of the county. One of the commonest later developments of the Mancroft style is best seen at East Harling; a rather different version, which also occurs at Mancroft, is also seen at Pulham St. Mary the Virgin, Martham and Mulbarton, and yet another sub-group within the Norwich style is listed under Cley. This by no means exhausts the variations within the locally-made glass and there are also important collections at Harpley, Wiggenhall St. Mary Magdalen and elsewhere, which were probably not made in Norwich.

In the 16th century glass, as at Shelton, Outwell, Norwich St. Andrew's and St. Stephen's, the late Gothic styles and the new renaissance realism, with its own distinctive decorative motifs, appear in various combinations, but generally show a lowering of quality compared with most of the 15th century work and the best English 16th century glass, which benefited more from the influx of Continental (mainly Flemish) artists and ideas.

The subject matter (iconography) of Norfolk glass has often been discussed before and there is not room here for more than a few general comments: the range and different types of subject will emerge in the course of the rest of the book. We must always remember that what we are seeing today is always incomplete, nearly always tracery figures, and that the glass in the main lights below was often of higher quality and more complex subject matter. To some extent the gaps in our knowledge can be filled by a study of the many documents which record the iconography of some at least of the lost glass. Some of these records and the surviving glass itself also reveal that although the windows of a church were often glazed piece-meal by various donors and workshops, and thus had rather arbitrary selections of subjects, there are cases in Norfolk, such as Elsing in the mid-14th century, Salle and Wiggenhall St. Mary Magdalen in the 15th century and Shelton in the 16th century, where the whole church, or large parts of it, seem to have been glazed according to an overall iconographic programme.

Moving away from the more art-historical aspects of style and iconography, we must consider for a moment another very necessary side to the study of stained glass, the elucidation of its historical context. When was it made? Who made it? Who paid for it? What was the reason behind the choice of subject? Many factors come into play here: the evidence of the glass itself, which may contain heraldry, figures of the donors or inscriptions giving their names and sometimes their dates; records of the glass in a more complete condition are again of considerable help here. The dates of the building of the church as revealed by the architecture and documents such as wills are also important; wills, moreover, also tell us to what saints or feasts the altars, images, and lights in the church were dedicated, which helps to explain the subject matter of the glass - the figure of the Holy Trinity at Ringland, for example, was originally in the east window of the north aisle, over the altar used by the Guild of the Holy Trinity. Generally speaking, whichever aspect of a medieval church we are looking at, we should always bear in mind the possible significance of all the other parts.

There has been room in this introduction to mention only a few of the more important factors in the study of stained glass; many further examples will be found in the main body of the text. There is just one further point to consider: the aesthetic quality of the glass. Stained glass has often been neglected in this country by art-historians, partly because of the physical difficulties involved in getting to see the widely dispersed and fragmentary surviving remains, and partly because, in the 15th century, from which most of our glass comes, English art is considered to have been in a period of decline, eclipsed by the brilliant achievements of Italy and Flanders. To the first problem, there is only one answer - go and have a look. To the second, several answers may be given, concerning Norfolk stained glass. First, there is very little of bad quality and most is of higher quality than much of the provincial art from other parts of England, and also on the continent; second, there is a handful of local works which are definitely of good quality - the glass at Narborough, North Tuddenham, St. Peter Mancroft and West Rudham, and the remains of the chancel glazing at Salle, stand comparison with the best glass of the period in any country. Lastly, it should be remembered that the almost superhuman feats of realistic painting and illusion of Van Eyck and his successors were not a suitable mode of expression for the essentially two-dimensional medium of stained glass, in which a clear, simple statement of the subject was vital for the didactic function of the glass and inherent in the nature and technique of the medium.

Tour 1

Stody

The glass in the north nave windows here is rather fragmentary and dirty, but of quite high quality. In the westernmost window is a series of kings and prophets or patriarchs, with no labels or symbols to identify them, apart from the arrow held by one of the kings, indicating that he is St. Edmund, and that therefore the kings are English, and not, as at Combs in Suffolk, for example, part of a genealogy of Christ. The presence of the prophets or patriarchs is interesting, and may have been paralleled at St. Peter Mancroft, Norwich, where the glass in the east window tracery now includes a series of English sainted kings, and the names of Asa and Isaac from a genealogy. The Mancroft kings are similar in design, but of less refinement than the rather elegant figures here. The next window contains part of a series of Apostles, and the remains of a Coronation of the Virgin in the same style. The broken figures in the east window of the south transept are in a slightly different style, and similar in their convoluted drapery to the related sets of female saints discussed under **Cley**. Parts of four saints can be discerned: Catherine (wheel and sword), Margaret (staff and dragon), Mary Magdalene (holding long hair), and, probably, Helen (cross). In the eighteenth century, the following saints were also recorded here in the glass: three bishops including St. Nicholas, St. Etheldreda, St. Lucy, St. Christopher, and (probably) St. George. Linnell compares this church with St. Peter Hungate, Norwich, for which there is a date of 1460 for the architecture, and this date would be about right for the glass here.

Bale

Although the church is dedicated to All Saints, there seems to have been a particular devotion to the Annunciation here. It appears from the surviving glass leaded into a south window that there were many representations of this event in the tracery lights (two Gabriels and four Marys are extant), and at least one main-light representation, which is now the main feature of the glazing. Repetition of scenes was common in medieval churches, but here there must have been some special reason. Figures of feathered angels, some playing musical instruments, account for much of the other glass, but there is also part of a main-light figure of an Apostle bearing a Creed scroll, and a panel of fragments (bottom centre) including part of an abbess, a figure of Christ Crucified from a Trinity representation, *Edwardi,* probably the name of a saint or donor, and pieces of early fourteenth century oak-leaf and acorn pattern work (grisaille), the oldest glass in the window. All the other glass so far mentioned, dates from c. 1450 - 80. Another exception is the central pair of figures; these are from the second half of the fourteenth century and represent prophets from a series holding Messianic texts, of which those here are from 1 Samuel XIV. 13, and Daniel IX. 26. The figures stand in contemporary canopy work. A small bust of the Risen Christ, of similar date, has also been leaded into this panel. Many of the pieces here have remains of the original border and background of rod-and-leaf and rose-en-soleil quarries. Notice the following technical points: first, the difference between the smear shading of the fourteenth century prophets and the stipple shading of the fifteenth century figures (the latter is more subtle and allows the light through better); second, the use of the same cartoon (full size pattern) for some of the Annunciation panels; lastly, the abrasion of the pattern on the red glass of the large Virgin Mary's mantle to show the clear glass beneath, red or ruby glass being made of two layers, one of ruby, the other of clear glass.

Field Dalling

Most of the medieval glass here is in the south nave windows, whose traceries contain the remains of three different series of figures of c. 1460-80. The easternmost has a series of female saints (see under **Cley**), of which the first is unidentifiable, and the others are Mary Magdalene,

Catherine, Agnes and Cecilia. The next window held eight of the twelve Apostles, of which we now recognise Andrew, Thomas, Jude, Philip, Bartholomew and Paul, all with their normal emblems. It is unfortunate that the third window retains the least of its original glazing, as its subject matter is rather more unusual than the other two. It seems to have had a set of sainted ecclesiastics, the first of which we see now is an abbess with a crozier - probably St. Etheldreda of Ely; next, after a lost figure, is possible St. Leger, and the last two figures are St. Giles and very likely St. Sylvester. These three male saints all appear in glass at Wiggenhall St. Mary Magdalene. The tracery of the middle window of the north aisle contains very restored and possibly rather earlier glass, being the remnants of two sets of figures which often appear together in late medieval art, namely, the Apostles carrying scrolls with portions of the Creed and the Prophets with Messianic texts. It is interesting to note and contrast the two radically different types of restoration represented here: the 'purist' one on the south, with clear glass where old glass is lost, and the attempt on the north side at a complete 'restoration', with the missing sections repainted. The first method is archaeologically more acceptable, the second, if well done, more pleasing aesthetically.

Glandford

The church here was totally restored in 1896 - 1906 by Sir Alfred Jodrell, and almost completely glazed with stained glass by Kempe and his pupil Ernest Heasman. The work of the latter artist, seen here, at **Salle, Letheringsett,** Holt, and many other places, has previously been attributed to Bryans, but this is a mistake. Heasman was a pupil of Kempe who was later employed as chief

draughtsman and designer by a Mr. Bryans, a businessman who owned a stained glass workshop, but who was not an artist or craftsman. Kempe was responsible for the east windows of both chancel and aisle, and Heasman for the other windows. The subjects shown in the glass here are briefly listed in the guide; a few details may be added. In the east window, the Virgin Mary holds the text of the beginning of the Magnificat - *Magnificat anima mea Dominum* (Luke 1, 46), normally associated with the Visitation, but here used as a general expression of praise to God, parallel to that held by St. Martin in the opposite light - *Venite exultemus Domino iubilemus* (Psalm XCIV in the Vulgate, verse 1). A more medieval derivation for the arrangement of the subject matter is seen in the east window of the north chapel, where the prophets in the architecture above the Annunciation scene recall the lay-out of the medieval *Biblia Pauperum* and other block books. The inscriptions they bear are Messianic texts from Isaiah VII, 14 and Numbers IV, 17. Another Old - New Testament link is seen in the adjacent window. The basic scheme is a figure of the Virgin carrying a book with the Magnificat text, flanked by personifications of Justice

Plate I Glandford

and Peace. If we recall that the text here often accompanies the Visitation, it is interesting that just such a combination of Visitation and Virtues occurs in more extended form at **Salle** in medieval glass restored by Heasman and others, over a completely new Jesse window by the same artist. A direct borrowing is indicated, though the Glandford rebuilding is a little earlier than the **Salle** restoration. The style of the two artists is clearly distinguishable; Kempe's glass is more sumptuous, with a fondness for jewelled effects and pearly borders, and the colours are richer. Heasman's shows a more thorough-going attempt to reproduce the style of English fifteenth century glass-painting, with the result that his technique is simpler, and his palette more subdued. In fact, whereas much Victorian glass is marred by an excess of dark colours, Heasman's windows, while possessing a limpid quality, are rather pale for some tastes. Both artists maintained a high level of technical competence - their work is notably more refined than the more admired Pre-Raphaelite glass of the middle of the nineteenth century, whose quality rests more on the powerful designs provided by some of the best artists of the day.

Cley

Apart from a few insignificant fragments arranged in a very curious fashion in a north chancel window and one or two pieces in the clerestory, the only old glass here is in the window to the left of the south door. The tracery of this window contains the best preserved example of a group of sets of female saints which can be seen in several churches in Norfolk, mostly in the

north of the county. The series here has the following saints: Agatha; Sitha?; a saint bearing a sword or stake based on the same cartoon as a figure at **Wighton**; Petronilla; probably Barbara; Faith; Agatha; Cecilia. Most of these saints appear in one or more of the other similar series at **Field Dalling**, **Wighton**, Martham and **Stody** and a lost series at Sharrington had six or seven female saints; Woodforde's conclusion was that the firm responsible for them had a set list of holy women which was varied according to the space available. This may be so, but it does not explain the original choice of saints, nor why a series of female saints was set up in a particular church. There is slight evidence at Cley concerning both these points and suggesting some element of patronal selection. In connection with the presence of St. Petronilla, it is worth noting that Petronilla de Nerford was the wife of William de Nerford, who held a manor in Cley in the 13th century and whose arms are among those carved on the porch. The chapel she owned at Little

Plate II Cley

Wenham, in Suffolk, has a roof boss bearing a figure of St. Petronilla. Also, we know from Cley wills that there was a guild of maidens in the church here, whose presence may account for the existence of the particular subject matter here, and possibly elsewhere. Stylistically, the Cley figures, along with those at the above-mentioned places, and also at the Burrell Collection in Glasgow and the Metropolitan Museum in New York (of unknown provenance), form an interesting group, not all by the same hand, but using common design sources and characterised by a particular type of voluminous drapery, with many rounded and convoluted folds, and by the relatively soft shading of the faces, with large round eyes. All this suggests a date in the 1430's at first sight, but the historical and architectural evidence points to the 1460's.

Kelling

Three panels from tracery lights have been leaded into the main lights of a south window. They represent three standing figures of crowned female saints, two of whom are also dressed as abbesses and carry croziers and books. There are no labels or emblems, but it is quite probable that the two similar figures are meant to be St. Etheldreda and St. Withburga. St. Anna, King of the East Angles, who died in battle in 654, was father of five saints, four of them daughters, of which two, those mentioned above, were associated with this part of the country, Etheldreda being the patroness of Ely, and St. Withburga having been abbess of Dereham. The two sisters appear together on the screens at Barnham Broom, Burlingham St. Andrew and Oxburgh (now in East Dereham church) and were recorded together with their sister Sexburga, queen of Kent, and also an abbess, in the glass at Walpole St. Peter. The third figure here is more of a problem, as many female saints were given royal attributes. A possible candidate is St. Helen, also a saint with (rather vague) East Anglian connections, being, according to legend, daughter of King Coel, of Colchester. She appears with Etheldreda on the screens at Horsham St. Faith and Upton, and in glass at **Salle**, Blythburgh in Suffolk and several other places in England. Normally, as at **Salle**, she holds a large wooden cross as her emblem. The condition of the figures makes a stylistic dating difficult - they probably were made somewhere around the middle of the 15th century.

Letheringsett

The window by the reading desk in the chancel contains two made-up panels of fragments of Norfolk medieval glass. As the guide says, it is of unknown provenance, but it is recorded in 1820 as being in a small building called 'The Hermitage' in the hall gardens, and was later in a summer house. Several of the figured pieces in the left panel - a head of God the Father and three musical angels - appear to date from c. 1430 - 40, but the angel's head bottom right is rather later. Note also a hand carrying a basket of loaves, almost certainly from a figure of St. Philip, and next to it, part of a crozier or cross staff. The main fragments in the other panel are two fifteenth century heads, large eyelet fillings, and a shield of arms. The church was drastically restored in the nineteenth century by William Butterfield and new stained glass was provided for many of the windows in the early years of this century, Sir Alfred Jodrell being a patron, as at **Salle** and **Glandford**. The guide says that the aisle windows are by Kempe, but comparisons with the glass in the two other churches mentioned indicate that his pupil Heasman (see **Glandford**) was also involved, and some windows are clearly by neither painter, being of inferior quality. Two windows are in Kempe's style - the east window of the south aisle, and the window in the north nave wall. As at **Glandford** we can see that of the two, Heasman was more concerned with a medieval approach. The former of Kempe's windows, an Annunciation, has a rather uncomfortable combination of an English fifteenth century type canopy framing a realistic interior with coffered ceiling, more after the manner of Flemish painting. Heasman's two windows - the two in the south aisle wall - are by contrast more medieval in spirit, texture and detail, down to the small figures of prophets standing in niches in the canopy shafting, such as are found in old glass at **Litcham** and Cawston. Beneath his New Testament figures he has placed seated prophets holding corresponding Old Testament texts: (from right to left) Malachi III, 1, Ezekiel XVI, 40, Isaiah LVII, 7, Psalm XVIII, 5. Again, this is medieval in conception, if not quite the usual thing in medieval glass as it survives in this part of the country.

Tour 2

Great Snoring

Here we have the remains of what must have been a very attractive small-scale fifteenth century series of the Nine Orders of Angels, such as was to be seen in many Norfolk churches, for example at **Banningham** and Narborough. The best pieces are in a south chancel window. The first tracery light has an angel playing a lute. The second opening has another feathered angel in the same style, but this one holds a pair of scales, the attribute of the Order Thrones. Next is a fine figure of an angel in armour, which has a wreathed bascinet on its head and a blue surcoat over the body. This represents the Order Powers, for, as at **Salle**, it carries a birch with which it subdues a devil, here done in ruby and shown with tied hands. The following angel, feathered and wearing a white robe, has no such distinguishing attribute, but is labelled *D(omi)nac(i)ones* (Dominations). The central main light has in the head a bust of an angel and also the word *Cherubin*, from the Order Cherubim. Another demi-figure of an angel holding a scroll bearing *Sanctus* is not a member of the Orders. The fragments in the border to this light include part of an angel standing on an axle with wheels, and this may well be part of the Orders series (c.f. **Harpley**). Hung against the east window are parts of other tracery lights with angels - the first and third have only a small part of the figure; the second and fifth are musical angels playing harp and lute; the fourth figure is of an angel with hands raised and wearing a scarf, similar to the one at Narborough where, as in this same panel, there is also part of an angel painted on ruby glass - the Order Seraphim. As Woodforde has pointed out, it is impossible to be sure of the identification of many angels from an Orders series, as the attributes given them vary a great deal. However, we can at least be certain here of the figures still retaining their labels.

East Barsham

A window in the centre of the north nave wall contained until recently beautiful but sadly broken and decayed glass; fortunately it has been removed for restoration, and will probably be replaced some time in 1975. Most of the glass is from the tracery, which has rather long central lights; so that the figures contained in them are almost the size of main light figures. They are two females, standing facing each other, with no label or obvious attribute, but the pose and costume (the veil of the left figure) indicate that they represent St. Elizabeth and the Virgin Mary respectively, and that the subject is the Visitation, one of the simplest, but most touching and human of the many religious scenes portrayed in medieval art. The same scene at St. Peter Mancroft, Norwich, is perhaps the most beautiful of all the panels there. Here, it is flanked by two musical angels, one blowing a trumpet, and the other playing a harp. The outer eyelets retain parts of their original 'pod' decoration, and the heads of the main lights have many pinnacled canopy tops. There are also fragments in the borders, and a piece of canopy work in the adjacent window. The elegant pose of the female figures and the drawing and arrangement of the flowing but bulky drapery, is similar to the connected groups of smaller female saints discussed under **Cley**.

South Creake

The glass here has been rearranged in fairly recent years and we cannot be sure of the original position of the rather fragmentary remains. The restorer has painted new glass for certain missing pieces, easily recognisable for the most part by its rather ghostly appearance. The majority of the glass is in four of the north aisle windows. The west window has as its centre piece a good figure of Christ in Majesty, wearing green robe and white mantle, of c. 1330-40. Most of the other pieces in the window, apart from a fourteenth century wheel from beneath an angel, are fifteenth century glass, including small angels and patterned quarries. One or two pieces in a tracery light have a border fitting the curve of the opening, indicating a fifteenth century reglazing of a fourteenth century window. The adjacent window has fifteenth century glass: a mostly restored fifteenth century small Trinity in the top tracery opening, with a row of six angels beneath; in the main lights, very disarranged canopy tops and broken and made-up figures, the best of which is the central figure of an Apostle from a series carrying articles of the Creed, of which two more figures are in the first light of the next window but one. That in the first window bears the scroll of St. James the Less and has part of his name beneath. The other pair of figures is St. James Major, with pilgrim's hat and staff (part of St. Andrew's text has been inserted in his) and St. Andrew, with saltire cross and his own text. These two figures are matched in the third light by a pair of female saints in the same style - St. Helen with cross, crown and book, and St. Agatha, with breast held by pincers, and a book. The centre light contains a mostly modern representation of the Trinity above a pair of angels with scrolls. Below is a kneeling female figure before a prayer desk. The tracery has four angels and the heads of the main lights contain fairly complete canopy tops. The east window of this aisle has some good pieces of glass of c. 1330-40, including censing angels and canopy tops. The top tracery light has a good fifteenth century female head. The central feature of the window is a now rather bizarre Crucifixion. The head and arms of Christ are fourteenth century glass, the rayed background is new glass in fifteenth century style, the date of the angel above; the body and legs are also in new glass and the hill of Calvary is made up of pieces of fourteenth century drapery. The east window of the other aisle has broken fragments of censing angels and other pieces of the same fourteenth century date and the north clerestory contains several fifteenth century demi-figures of angels. The style of the fifteenth century aisle glass is unusual, being rather sketchy and uncertain in drawing, without the assurance of the typical 'Norwich School' glass.

Burnham Deepdale

Fragments of old glass have been leaded into six windows here. A list is unavoidable: vestry east window - fourteenth and fifteenth century fragments, of which the most interesting may be part of an heraldic border, bearing argent, a saltire engrailed sable. Many heraldic devices, such as fleur-de-lys, were used in the fourteenth century as border decoration without any implied connection with a particular family. An example of a border with a connection is recorded at **Elsing,** where the portraits of Sir Hugh and Lady Margery Hastings were edged with their own blazon. The fragments here, not being amongst the usual repertoire of quasi-heraldic border patterns, may have referred to a specific family. The best piece in the west window of the north aisle is a roundel of the Trinity, of mid-fifteenth century date, and similar in style to that at Thurton. Figures of the Trinity, ranging in size from this to full-length main-light representations, such as at **Ringland**, were common in medieval glass. There is also part of a figure of a nimbed queen with arrows - probably St. Ursula - of later date, and rose-en-soleil quarries, an IHC roundel, parts of musical angels, the word *Gelda* (indicating a window provided by a guild) and a merchant's mark. A tiny window by the pulpit has a few insignificant fragments, but the west tower window has parts of censing angels and most of a figure of St. Mary Magdalene, unfortunately inside out. Finally, the two porch windows are glazed with old pieces and a modern inscription. Note the representation of the moon, which would have originally accompanied a fifteenth century Crucifixion, along with one of the sun.

Warham St. Mary

The foreign glass here must claim most of our attention, but do not miss the collection of delightful fragments of English glass leaded into a north window. These include, in rather brown fourteenth century glass, the Angel of the Expulsion, Adam Delving and Eve Spinning from a Creation series. The majority of the other fragments are of the fifteenth century. The most interesting of the foreign glass is in the east window of the chancel, the tracery and heads of which contain broken glass, including the words *Orige* and *Nuncius* from a now widely dispersed Life of St. Barbara series, one panel of which is in St. Stephen's church, Norwich, and part of a

Tour 2

saint in armour, who is identifiable as St. Gerlachus, from window 13 of the Steinfeld glass, 1534 (see introduction and **Erpingham**). Five of the main light panels are from this same source: the Transfiguration, from window 10, 1530; Christ's Farewell to His Mother, and His Entry into Jerusalem, from window 11, c. 1530 - 31; the Betrayal of Christ (based on a woodcut from Durer's Little Passion of 1511); and the Descent from the Cross, from window 19, 1540. The sixth panel, an Entombment of Christ, is French sixteenth century work. Perhaps the best known German sixteenth century cloister glazing scheme is that of the Cistercian monastery of Altenberg, near Cologne, painted during the first third of the sixteenth century, and illustrating the life of St. Bernard, the founder of the order. Many panels from this series are extant, though now widely dispersed - several are in St. Mary's, Shrewsbury, and another is in Marston Bigot church, Somerset. A few panels were lost in the last war in Germany. A photograph of one lost panel shows the Virgin with the Child, sheltering under her cloak members of the Cistercian order, kneeling monks on the left, nuns on the right. However, the general appearance of the glass on this photograph would lead one to have doubts about its authenticity and these

Plate III Warham St. Mary

are confirmed when one looks at a panel in the south-east chancel window here which shows just this scene in an identical arrangement, but rather broken, and with the figure of the Virgin missing. This glass is definitely sixteenth century in date and must be the original, the destroyed panel having been a copy. Another previously unrecognised panel from this series is in the St. Peter Hungate Museum, Norwich. Most of the other glass in the chancel windows is sixteenth century French work and the fine figure of King David (the head is new) in the west window is sixteenth century Cologne work. A monumental inscription here tells us that W. H. Langton, rector, who died in 1836, "adorned the church with painted glass". It is very probable that the foreign glass (and perhaps the English) came from J.C. Hampp of Norwich (see introduction and **Erpingham**).

Wighton

Apart from some eyelets in a north aisle window, the medieval glass is confined to the four east and west aisle windows. That in the eastern pair has received the attention of a restorer - one

12

whose work is often seen in Norfolk - and in the north window he has painted new heads and wings for the two angels holding texts, and new heads for the centre pair of the four female saints above in the tracery. It is interesting that his work is also much in evidence at Martham, where similar angels with scrolls appear, and there is a very restored figure based on the same cartoon as the more complete figure of St. Martha or St. Juliana here. The four saints are difficult to identify positively. The well preserved figure in the first light carries a sword or stake and may be one of a number of saints. It is based on the same cartoon as a figure at **Cley**, and this set of saints appears to be from the same workshop as the **Cley** saints, and other female saints at Martham are rather similar. The second figure as restored shows St. Catherine, the third, with a devil on a chain, may be St. Martha or St. Juliana, and the last, St. Agatha with a flesh-hook, is also based on the same design as a rather better version at **Cley**. The four male figures in the south-east window, are four of the Apostles, St. Paul?, St. Andrew, St. Bartholomew, and St. Peter, and are by the same workshop as the first window. Here again, parts are restored, including most of the canopy work. The two western windows contain fifteenth century figures of angels, those on the south playing rebecs, and those on the north, mere fragments, stand on wheels, as at **Colby** and St. Peter Hungate, Norwich, for example.

Plate IV Wighton

Great Walsingham

The number of windows here retaining fragments of original fourteenth century glass indicates an extensive original scheme. Perhaps the most interesting window is that at the east end of the north aisle. Its tracery glazing illustrates the difficulties caused for the glazier by the irregular and often rather small shapes of curvilinear tracery. Often, the only recourse was to foliage decoration (as in other windows here), but in this case, as at Barton Mills, in Suffolk, grotesques have been used to fill some of the lesser openings and there is also the unusual feature of a scene represented only by the head and hands of the participants. The Coronation of the Virgin is one of the most instantly recognisable subjects - the inclination of the Virgin's head, with hands in a prayerful attitude, and the raised hand of Our Lord being almost all that is necessary to indicate it - and is just what we find here. The opposite window in the south aisle also has a pair of heads in the tracery, probably Apostles, and another north aisle window has a small figure of Christ displaying the sacred wounds. All the aisle windows retain vestiges of decorative glazing in the tracery and a variety of motifs is to be seen - oak leaf and maple leaf and hawthorn diaper, for example, and the differences in treatment indicate that perhaps more than one atelier was at work here. This is confirmed also by marked differences between the canopy tops in the first south window from the east, and the 'Coronation' window. The former use much more coloured glass and have little idea of perspective and would appear to date from c. 1320 - 40. The latter have much more white glass, side-turned buttresses (also a grotesque, unusual in a canopy) and would date more probably from c. 1340 - 60.

Tour 3

Stratton Strawless

The Marsham family has had a long association with this church and in 1473 John Marsham left money in his will to the glazing of a north window. Two of the north windows retain their medieval glazing in the tracery - can either of these be the window paid for by John Marsham? Blomefield describes what must be the main-light panels, including figures of the donor and wife, and of St. Catherine and St. Margaret and the Coronation of the Virgin. These sacred subjects, plus the Annunciation, appear in this order in the more westerly window, but in the tracery, and perhaps repeat the iconography below. The style of the glass of this window, in comparison with the softer but more monumental painting of that of the next window, also suggests that this is the later and more likely of the two to be associated with the Marsham bequest. The second window contains a fine series of the Four Evangelists, portrayed as seated and winged figures, labelled and accompanied by their symbols (that of St. Matthew is missing). St. Luke is shown in his role as an artist, following the legend that he painted the portrait of the Virgin Mary. Each of the two windows has its own type of canopy in the heads of the main lights. The single head in one of these lights is a good example of local work of the third quarter of the fifteenth century. The windows of the south aisle contain a few English and foreign fragments of various dates.

Plate V Stratton Strawless

Hevingham

Here is another church containing panels from the sixteenth century cloister glazing of the monastery of Steinfeld (see introduction and **Erpingham**). This collection, now arranged in a south nave window, also contains fragments of earlier English glass in the tracery, but is mainly interesting because, unlike the other collections of Steinfeld glass in Norfolk, it is made up of smaller scenes from the original tracery lights and heads of the main lights, consisting of Old and New Testament scenes and characters which relate to the Life of Christ series in the main register. Not all the pieces here can definitely be linked with Steinfeld, and some are very difficult to see. The most important are: 1. The two lozenges with male busts; these represent Melchior, on the left, and Caspar, on the right, with the shields traditionally ascribed to them in the middle ages, and were to be seen, together with the third Magus, in the truncated 4th window of the Steinfeld cloisters, glazed in c. 1525. 2. The Spies and the Grapes, and 3. Naaman washing in the Jordan, from window 9, c. 1529. 4. Abraham and the Three Young Men, from window 10,

1530. 5. Abraham washing the Three Young Men's feet, from window 12, c. 1531 - 33. 6. David crossing the Brook Cedron, and 7. St. Mark fleeing the Soldiers, from window 13, 1534. 8. The Sacrifice of Isaac, from window 18, 1539 - 40. The divergence in style and quality between these panels, which are all from the same glazing scheme, is caused by the length of time over which the glass was made, and also by the fact that some of the pieces, notably the last mentioned, have been rather drastically restored. The latin inscription below tells us that this window was provided by H. P. Marsham in 1881. For the earlier history of this glass, see the entry on **Erpingham**.

Erpingham

Apart from a panel of local fifteenth century glass showing an angel (head new) carrying a trumpet, which is in the east window of the south aisle, all the medieval glass here is in the east chancel window, whose main lights contain a fine collection of twelve German and French panels. The eight lower panels are all from the cloister glazing of the monastery of Steinfeld, in the Eifel region of Germany, and represent the largest collection of glass from this source outside the Victoria and Albert Museum, London, which has thirty-eight panels. Bottom row: 1. Adoration of the Child, with Shepherds, from window 3, c. 1524. 2. Christ's Appearance to St. Thomas, and 3. to the Three Marys, both from window 21, 1542. 4. The Flight into Egypt, with part of the Massacre of the Innocents, from window 7, 1528. Middle row: 5. St. Quirinus, from window 19. 1540; only the figure in this and number 8. are original. 6. Lower half: St. Paul and St. Norbert, from window 5, 1526; upper half: mostly modern, but contains a small scene of the martyrdom of St. Quirinus from the same panel as number 5. 7. Lower half: The Virgin Mary and St. Potentinus, from window 5, 1526. 8. St. Quirinus again, this time from window 16, 1538. The two Quirinus panels are definitely identifiable in a sale catalogue of 1804 of glass imported by the German-born Norwich merchant, Johann Christoph Hampp, which proves

Plate VI Erpingham

that, as has been previously suggested, at least some, if not all the Steinfeld glass was brought to this country by him.   Panels 1 - 4 come from the long series of the Life of Christ made for the upper register of the main lights, the other four panels are from the lower register which mainly held figures of donors (some of which survive in this county at Chedgrave and **Mulbarton**) and saints connected with the monasteries of the Eifel region. The nearby monastery of Mariawald also had glass of the early 16th century, which was imported into England in the 19th century, and the Adoration of the Child scene in the Victoria and Albert Museum from there is based on the same design as the same scene here in panel 1. Top row: 9. This is French sixteenth century glass and probably shows a scene from the story of Susannah and the Elders. 10. and 11. are also French, but from the second half of the fifteenth century, and show the Presentation of the Virgin Mary, and Joachim and St. Anne. 12. This is a German sixteenth century panel with the Massacre of the Innocents. It is rather alarming that the brown corrosion evident on 10. and 11. has occurred since the glass was installed here in 1958. The glass was brought from Blickling Hall, where it had previously been in a staircase window.

Sustead

The glass here is a good example of one of the frustrations of looking at medieval glass painting in England, for as in so many places we have a few shattered remains of what must have been quite high quality work. Only the tracery of two south nave windows retains any original glazing. First window: a female saint carrying a book - her flared cuffs were an early fifteenth century fashion - and a figure of St. Catherine with her usual wheel and sword. This window probably contained a series of female saints, though of earlier date by a decade or two than the other series mentioned under **Cley** which date apparently from the 1460's. The next window had a series of musical angels, and still to be seen are figures of one playing a lute, with delicately drawn sound hole, and plectrum, and of another playing the bagpipes. This latter is a delightful figure - note the rich, intricately painted drapery, and the lion's head at the join of pipe and bag. Although generally speaking the amount of coloured glass used in a window was governed by economic factors, in the fifteenth century, as here, we do find high quality glass with very little coloured glass, perhaps a reflection of the characteristic English love of detailed drawing on glass. It is interesting to note that the architectural and sculptural details of the previous century are also here of surprisingly high quality for such a small church.

Colby

Apart from one or two fragments in the south windows, all the glass here was leaded into the east window by G. Coleby, Rector, in 1825. The top quatrefoil contains a pelican pecking her breast to feed her young with her own blood - a symbol of our Lord's Passion, indicating, if it is in situ, that the main subject of the window was probably a Crucifixion. The other figures in the tracery are parts of a series, or possibly two, of the Twelve Apostles. We can recognise St. Peter, St. John the Evangelist, St. Jude, St. Andrew and St. Matthew or St. Thomas. The main lights contain part of yet another series (also from tracery lights) but of slightly better quality: top left and right, St. James Major and John the Evangelist, and bottom centre, St. Peter. The remaining figures are God the Father, from a Coronation of the Virgin, the Virgin Mary from an Annunciation and two angels standing on wheels (c.f. Ezekiel X). There are also two canopy tops, a rayed sun, an eagle and a rose-en-soleil. The rather piecemeal patronage prevalent in most parish churches in the fifteenth century, with single windows being given by different people over a period of time, meant that the duplication of subject matter, as here, was by no means uncommon. At Pulham St. Mary the Virgin, two sets of Apostles are still in evidence, for example. Occasionally, as with the Annunciations at **Bale** and the rebus at **Shelton**, the repetition was probably intentional. The style of the glass here is difficult to set in chronological perspective, but may suggest a date in the first half of the fifteenth century.

Banningham

Parts of a colourful and well-painted series of the Nine Orders of Angels are to be seen in the second window from the east in the south aisle. The first tracery figure is labelled *Seraphim* and wears purple feathers, and the next is a Cherub, again clothed in feathers, which here have eyes on them (Ezekiel X.12). In the first main light are fragments of an archangel holding a box containing flowers - an unusual emblem for this order. Although, as Woodforde has shown, the emblems given to the orders vary widely, the identification at Banningham is assured by the surviving labels. The other two tracery figures, probably in situ, represent two of the Four Evangelists, of which only the second is identifiable, as St. John. A figure of the same Evangelist at Ashill is from the same cartoon, but in a different, more linear and bold, style. Notice also the pod eyelets, very common in Norfolk, and a feature which can be paralleled in illuminated manuscripts of the period. Other fragments leaded into the main lights include pieces of fourteenth century leaf grisaille, parts of a fifteenth century donor inscription, Crucifixion and Ecce Homo, and an interesting detail of a church with belfry, of the same date. In the heads of the lights are richly detailed canopy tops. The easternmost north aisle window has some fifteenth century glass in the upper part, but apart from the figure of Gabriel in the Annunciation, pieces of the censing angels, and the central canopy top, the rest is restoration work.

Tour 4

Bawburgh

The shrine of St. Walstan was at Bawburgh before the Reformation and the resulting prosperity brought by pilgrims probably explains the rebuilding and redecoration of the chancel which seems to have occurred about 1309. The partly restored figures of two small censing angels in the large north window are possibly part of this work. The rest of the glass here is of the next century and the best pieces are in the opposite window, where a fairly complete figure of St. Barbara, holding palm and tower, stands next to the upper half of a Gabriel from an Annunciation. These two figures are in the same style, being very similar to the glass at **East Harling**, which dates from c. 1463 - c. 1480. The next window has glass by a different hand and in more fragmentary condition, but of about the same date, including part of the figure of the Virgin Mary from another Annunciation and of a female saint, possibly Catherine. The window facing has two canopy tops of like date. Of the remains in the north window not mentioned, the most interesting are a series of roundels bearing the text of the 'Nunc Dimittis'. The name of St. Gregory in the centre fragment panel may or may not belong to the head below wearing a Doctor's cap, but both pieces indicate the former presence of a series of the Four Doctors of the Church. The shield is made up from two broken coats of arms, which indicate a date after 1475, which is little earlier than the two large heads, possible from a large Coronation of the Virgin.

Ringland

Donor figures with names beneath normally allow us to discover the identity of the people who gave a window and thus some idea of its date, but in this case, none of the handful of names visible has yielded any concrete information. However, the mitre and initial W carved on the

Plate VII Ringland

roof suggest a date for the fifteenth century rebuilding in the episcopacy of Walter Lyhart, Bishop of Norwich, 1446 - 72, and a rough indication of the date of the glass is given by the similarity of the Ringland donors to those at Taverham, which can be dated on historical evidence to 1459 - 88 and probably c. 1466. Stylistically, too, a date in the 1460's would seem right, a period when, as here, the painting of figures is characterised by a sharpness of detail, with thin, pointed facial features and a rather fussy treatment of drapery with accessories. This is best seen in the large figures in the clerestory, which represent the Annunciation in two panels, the Holy Trinity (originally in the window at the east end of the north aisle, where the guild of the Holy Trinity had an altar), the Virgin and Child (another from here is in the Cathedral) and St. John the Baptist. Such a collection of main light figures is a rare survival in Norfolk. Note also the carefully drawn but faded roundels above, bearing sacred monograms and the symbols of the Evangelists, and also the beautiful centaur roundel in the south aisle. This relates in subject matter and style to the famous East Anglian illuminated manuscripts of the first half of the fourteenth century, whose margins often were peopled with such grotesques. The closest comparison is with the Ormesby Psalter of c. 1310 - 25.

Weston Longville

The glass here cannot compete in interest with the fine Jesse Tree wall painting of about 1350 - 1370, or the Apostles with Creed Scrolls painted on the screen. The only remains are in the tracery lights of two south aisle windows. The easternmost has in the second and fifth main openings partly restored figures of musical angels of typical Norwich workmanship. The head and part of the left wing and background of the left figure are new, and that on the right has been given a robe, when originally it would have had feathered legs. One angel plays a lute and the other a harp. Although of the simplest and cheapest type of fifteenth century figured glazing, this glass still maintains a standard of painting which is higher than much of the screen painting and some of the manuscript painting of the period. The third window from the east again has old glass in three of the tracery lights. The fourth light has a figure which has been restored, probably correctly, to represent St. John the Evangelist; the fifth contains a figure of St. James the Great, shown with pilgrim's staff and hair shirt decorated with whelks, and not the more usual scallop shells; the sixth is of St. Philip, holding both a basket of loaves and some larger loaves. These Apostles are similar to those at **Field Dalling** and **Wighton,** and are linked stylistically with the series of female saints at these places and elsewhere, discussed under **Cley.** This link is strengthened by the fact that the figure of.St. James here is identical to that in St. Peter Hungate, Norwich, which also has a figure of St. Agatha from a series of female saints, in turn from the same cartoon as the one at **Cley.** The historical evidence at St. Peter Hungate suggests a date of c. 1460 for the glass mentioned there, and this whole stylistic group seems to fall within the period c. 1460 - 80.

Elsing

Much blame has been attached to Puritan iconoclasm for the loss of our medieval painted glass. The following quotation from Thomas Martin's notes on this church shows a different aspect: "The East Window has been beautifully adorn'd with painting, and indeed so have all about ye church w(hich) were never broken by design, but suffer'd to fall to ruin by the Incuriousness of the Parishioners". We can reconstruct the scheme of the east window from old records. The bottom register had figures of Sir Hugh Hastings (d. 1347) and Margery Foliot, his wife, supporting a model of the church (which he built), with an English inscription beneath and shields on each side. The next row above contained five scenes, surmounted by tall canopies, from the Life of the Virgin Mary, to whom the church is dedicated; a sixth, Her Coronation, was in the tracery, along with more heraldry. Among the few fragments now in this window is the head of an ox, perhaps from the Nativity scene once in the second light. The rest of the old glass here is now in the two south chancel windows. The eastern light of the first has a medley of fragments, including what may be the original Virgin Mary from her Coronation in the east window, a shield with the Foliot arms, a censing angel and part of a Trinity. The other lights contain very restored figures of three Apostles, carrying Creed Scrolls - St. Matthew, St. Jude and St. Philip. The latter has been given the fuller's bat of St. James the Less in the restoration. The date of this glass is a problem - it has been put at c. 1375, but may well be earlier and part of the original mid-century glazing scheme.

Booton

A first visit to Booton church is always a remarkable experience, evoking feelings of delight, horror, even mirth, but never indifference. The church was rebuilt in the last century by the Rev. Whitwell Elwin and was finished in 1891. The architecture can only be described as a gothic fantasy, combining elements from various sources into a somewhat bizarre but striking whole. All the windows have stained glass of the period (or possibly a little later) and all contain representations of Angels, reflecting the dedication of the church to St. Michael and All Angels. As in so many nineteenth and early twentieth century glazing schemes, one gets the impression that the designer of the scheme started by imagining a strictly biblical or theological arrangement, but soon became carried away on flights of iconographical fancy. The subject matter of the chancel windows is fairly orthodox in conception. The east window has the common juxtaposition of Christ between the Virgin Mary and St. John the Evangelist, but not as a Crucifixion scene, as is more normal. As in all the tracery lights of the nave and chancel windows, those here contain winged putti heads; in the main lights Angels are represented by figures of St. Michael and two Archangels? in the lower register. The side windows of the chancel have a selection of Old and New Testament scenes including Angels: on the north, the Annunciations to the Virgin and to Zachariah, and the Angels appearing to Hagar in the Wilderness, and on the south, Christ and the Angel in the Garden of Gethsemane, with the Sacrifice of Isaac, and Abraham and the Three Young Men. When we reach the nave, any appearance of a rigid scheme seems to collapse. The three windows on each side are filled with a mass of figures processing towards the east. Those on the north side consist of Angels accompanying saints - those recognisable are martyrs: St. George, St. Ursula, St. Agnes. On the south side we see musical Angels, with the addition of the most famous of biblical musical characters, King David. These windows are lighter in tone than those of the chancel and the overall effect is of silvery blue, green and grey, with touches of bright red in contrast. The tower windows, again rather darker, have Angels accompanying children on the west, the Virgin and Child on the north and St. Anne? on the south. This accent on children and mothers plus the presence of a dove in each light of the windows, representative of the Holy Spirit, implies that the tower area is to be seen principally as a baptistry, the font being placed in the centre of it. In the vestry the windows have Angels with musical instruments and instruments of the Passion. The settings are simpler and the general effect one of lightness. According to a manuscript account by a member of the Elwin family, the designer of the Annunciation window in the chancel was a Mr. Buckley, of whom he speaks favourably. The rest of the chancel windows were mainly the responsibility of two glaziers called Purchase and Booker, and the latter of these was also in charge of the glazing of the rest of the church. About these two artists the writer speaks very scathingly. However, while some of the chancel windows have the best individual panels, the overall impression of the nave windows is remarkable, but the east window and other windows in the baptistry and vestry are not so convincing in terms of style or technique.

Salle

This glorious church has highly interesting glass of various periods. The earliest is in the south aisle, where one window has in the tracery two figures of God the Father, and below, fragments of inscription, all from an Old Testament series datable to c. 1411. The chancel was built about 1440, and retains part of its contemporary glazing. The figures in the east window are what remain of a sumptuous series of the Nine Orders of Angels, here represented in pairs, with no sparing of coloured glass (which was expensive), but without the extreme richness of colour and

Plate VIII Salle

ornament of the slightly later glass in the Beauchamp Chapel, Warwick, of 1447 - 49, commonly cited as the most lavish display of English fifteenth century glass, but lacking the good taste and elegance of the Salle glass. The Orders now to be seen are Archangels, standing on a building (the head is an insertion), Principalities, with kneeling kings, red demons (part of a Fall of the Rebel Angels) and Powers birching demons. The heraldry in this window indicates the involvement in this church of some very important families - the Delapoles, Bardolfs, Beauforts and also (but now lost) the Morleys and Brewes. This may explain the size of the church and the magnificence of its original furnishings. The figures of the prophets, patriarchs and cardinals in the tracery of the side windows are of high quality in their facial drawing and of great interest, because of the relationship between their subject matter and that of the lost glass of the main lights below, which had a series of Kings, Popes, and Bishops and Archbishops. The old glass in the north transept, also of the 1440's, is likewise of iconographical interest, although very restored. It is in the tracery over the excellent modern Jesse window by Heasman (see **Glandford**) and represents the Visitation accompanied by personifications of the meeting of Mercy and Truth, Justice and Peace, following Psalm 85, v.10, the text of which is on the scrolls they carry. The tracery of the east window of the north aisle now has a very restored Annunciation, but this may have originally been a Coronation of the Virgin Mary. The surviving panels in the south transept need some historical interpretation, for although the tracery of the east and south windows is clearly of the same period, these windows contain glass in two different styles, and that in the east window appears to have been made originally for tracery of a different shape. It includes figures of Thomas Briggs, who built the transept about 1444, his two wives Margaret, and what is presumably his patron saint, St. Thomas of Canterbury. The figures of St. Margaret and St. Catherine, in the chancel, also belong to this glass. That in the south window - angels and saints - is later in style, probably from the last quarter of the fifteenth century. What must have happened is that, for some unknown reason, only a few decades after the transept was built it was remodelled and the east and south windows given new tracery forms. Of the original glazing, some was kept, notably that relating to the original founder, and was adapted to suit the new tracery shapes, and new glass was made for the remaining openings.

Guestwick

A study of the available information on the glass here illustrates quite well the uses and limitations of antiquarian descriptions. Both Blomefield and Martin tell us quite a lot about the medieval glass as it was here in the eighteenth century. In the north aisle were at least three scenes, or series of scenes, probably in different windows. One contained the Martyrdom of St. Edmund, another, the Circumcision (presumably all that remained of a series of the Life of Christ), and a third, a scene of a corpse on a sea shore, with several people looking over it, a boat nearby, and the inscription beneath, *Hic iacet Corpus Jacobi sup. Collem.* The interpretation of this scene is fascinating, for the inscription is ambiguous. In the church is to be found the brass of James At Hille, of about 1520. The name in the inscription can be a Latin translation of this name, but the whole text can also mean 'Here lies the body of James on the Hill', and the scene described could very well represent one of the posthumous events in the Legend of St. James the Great. It may, of course, be intended to mean both. In the south aisle was more glass: first, scenes from a series of the Corporal Acts of Mercy, such as survive at Combs, in Suffolk, Tattershall, in Lincolnshire, and, more fully, All Saints, North Street, York, for example; second, figures of St. John the Baptist and St. John the Evangelist, with three shields of arms below, indicating a marriage which has not been identified, but the man was almost certainly called John. All this information would seem likely to provide a good start for the study of the surviving glass, which has been gathered together into the centre lights of two south aisle windows, but, for one good reason, it does not. That reason is that, as so often, the existing glass is largely from tracery lights, whereas the recorded glass would have been in main lights. However, a few pieces come from the larger main light scenes, notably the rather grotesque heads done in various colours. These may well be from the series of the Corporal Acts of Mercy, in which the various unfortunates being ministered unto are sometimes represented with rather twisted and discoloured features. The main items of the glazing are four more or less complete tracery figures of typical Norwich work of c. 1460 - 80. Those in the western window of the two are ? an apostle and a bishop; those in the eastern, a bishop (with an old man's head) and an almost whole figure of St. Catherine. Amongst the rest of the fragments, practically all of similar date and workmanship, note the canopy work, foliage eyelet filling, parts of musical angels playing shawm ? and harp, a piece with the Christ Child set on rays, probably from a Nativity, and part of a female saint with a dagger in her neck, St. Lucy.

Tour 5

Ketteringham

The central theme of the glazing of the tracery of the east window is the common combination of the Annunciation and Coronation of the Virgin Mary, which can be seen as an abbreviated form of her adult life. The earthly event is flanked by a row of saints, which should be read in pairs from the centre outwards: SS Edmund and John the Baptist, Margaret and Catherine, George and Michael (this latter not an earthly figure, but often paired with St. George at this period). The heavenly Coronation above is flanked by two pairs of angels. Although an example of a simple type of glazing, with little colour and simple backgrounds, this is an interesting scheme for the completeness of its condition and for its connections with other glass in Norfolk. The six-winged angel is from the same cartoon as one at Narborough, the harp-playing angel from one used at Great Cressingham and the Coronation from one used at **Stratton Strawless**. The interesting thing about these connections is that these other figures are not in the same style as their counterparts at Ketteringham, and, in fact, the Narborough glass appears to be more related to Midlands glass than that of East Anglia. The heraldry and remains of a figure in armour in the main lights connect this glass with a Sir Henry Grey, who lived here in the first half of the fifteenth century (and not later, as Blomefield thought). The many other pieces include other fragments, probably of the original glazing, and several English and Flemish roundels. A full list is not possible, but note more especially: top row, IHC monogram, St. Christopher; second row, St. John the Baptist, a hen with *rey* on a scroll (a rebus for Henrey), part of a large figure of an archbishop, the head having been replaced by a roundel, a plant on a barrel (a rebus for Thistleton ?, or perhaps Carlton), St. Anne with the Virgin and Child; third row, St. James ? the Great, an archbishop, St. Barbara, and a seated, crowned figure playing a psaltery.

Mulbarton

As at Salle, the south aisle of Martham church originally had an Old Testament series in its windows. 'Eve Spinning' from this glazing can still be seen there, but two of the panels were brought to this church in the early nineteenth century by a curate of Martham who obtained the living here. They represent part of the Expulsion of Adam and Eve from the Garden of Eden, and 'Adam Delving'. The third figure in the east window shows Powers from the Orders of Angels and is also from Martham. The style of the fine heads of Adam here, which have grave, expressive features, but are painted in a soft, sketchy technique, can be recognised in other Norfolk glass, notably in two of the three panels in the east window of St. Peter Mancroft, Norwich, showing scenes from the Passion of Christ. This Passion Master, whose work seems to date around the 1460's, provides an interesting link between the softer and more naturalistic facial painting of the first half of the century, and the more linear and conventional-ised Norwich school head types of the second half, as seen in much of the later Mancroft glass. Of the other glass at Mulbarton, note the two figures in the south chancel window. One is a combination of parts of an earlier panel of St. Anne teaching the Virgin Mary to read, and a fifteenth century prophet or patriarch; the other is a King, holding a sceptre and a model church, possibly King Solomon, from a genealogy of Christ.

Saxlingham Nethergate

This church contains a collection of glass of several different periods, including the earliest known in a Norfolk church. Unfortunately, much of the glass is not in situ, and there is not space to describe it all in detail. There was an extensive restoration here in 1867, when a north aisle was added, but earlier photographs show that some of the glass here could not have fitted in date or shape any of the original windows, suggesting that it was brought in from another church. It may be relevant to this idea that in 1688 the parishioners of the other church in the village, Saxlingham Thorpe, were told to give up their church and come to worship here; any painted glass in the abandoned church would probably have been transferred at that time. This may have included the mid-thirteenth century glass now in two of the south chancel windows. In the easternmost, we see four slightly pointed medallions portraying, on the left, seated figures of St. John and St. James, and the Martyrdom of St. Edmund, and on the right, the beheading of an unknown saint,

Plate IX Saxlingham Nethergate

and St. Edmund offering up the arrows of his martyrdom to heaven. The patterned grey glass (grisaille) in the lower half of the adjacent window is of similar date, but the maple leaf grisaille between the medallions is of later date, probably early fourteenth century. Above the earlier grisaille are set two figures of Apostles - St. Philip and St. James the Less, clearly from tracery lights whose shape was not in any of the windows here. They date from c. 1350 - 90 and echo the style of some of the English manuscript painting of the period. The small south west window of the chancel has a c. 1500 roundel of the Virgin and Child with St. Anne, and below, what remains of two scenes, the Resurrection and the Nativity, originally in the tracery of the south east chancel window, and part of the same glazing scheme as that of the east window. The tracery of the east window has in situ but patched glass continuing and completing the Life of Christ (or perhaps of the Virgin Mary) series probably begun by the Nativity in the south east window. A Coronation of the Virgin is flanked by Pentecost on the left and the Ascension on the right. Of the glass now in the main lights of the east window, the three large shields and the roundels with IHC and M belong there; the former date the glass to c. 1390 - 1413. Of the fragmentary panels in the north chancel window, the top pair come from the tracery lights of a north nave window which had a central figure of Christ seated on a rainbow, with angels bearing Passion symbols to right and left, and censing angels in the side lights. The other pieces are what is left of a series of the Four Doctors of the Church; the figure of St. Jerome in his cardinal's hat has its own naive charm. All this glass is of the fifteenth century. The various panels leaded into the nineteenth century east window of the north aisle include canopy tops from the c. 1400 glazing scheme, small figures of a bishop, archbishop and king (Edward the Confessor) of similar date but unknown provenance, and two musical angels of perhaps c. 1420 - 50, possibly from the west tower window. Lastly, the renaissance shields of arms in the north east aisle window are of the same design as some in **Merton** church.

Bedingham

The east window of the north aisle has a modern arrangement of glass of various dates. The two outer lights contain in their heads attractive panels of early fourteenth century glass from the top of a pointed main light. Each shows the large crocketted finial which would have surmounted the canopy below, and each has a wide border typical of the period, on the left, consisting of a running vine leaf pattern, and on the right of fleurs-de-lys. The large conglomeration of painted glass in the central light contains some interesting small figures from tracery lights. The pair to left and right are from a set of Apostles with Creed Scrolls, the former bearing *Ascendit ad (caelos, sedet ad dexteram dei patris omnipotentis).* (He ascended into heaven: He sitteth at the right hand of the almighty Father), normally assigned to St. James the Less, but also part of St. Thomas' usual sentence - *(Descendit ad inferna, t)ercia die resur(rexit a mortuis)* (He descended into hell: on the third day he rose from the dead). The latter is identified as St. Philip by the basket of loaves he carries, and has part of his accustomed text: *Inde venturus (est iudicare vivos et mortuos)* (From whence he shall come to judge the living and the dead). The more complete central figure is of St. Catherine, but has been given a male head. These figures appear to date from the first half of the fifteenth century. The two large roundels in this window are late work done in a different technique from medieval glass, in that they use coloured enamels which are applied to the surface of the glass and fired to give adhesion, whereas the colour in medieval glass, apart from yellow stain, is in the glass itself. They represent the stoning of St. Stephen, and Saul on the road to Damascus.

Denton

Of all the patchworks of miscellaneous fragments in the windows of our Norfolk churches, this is perhaps the most exuberant, and in some ways the most interesting. It is in fact the earliest such arrangement in the county as far as we know (most were done in the first half of the nineteenth century), having been collected by the Rev. Postlethwaite, and arranged and leaded into the window by Joshuah Price in 1716 - 19. Price was a well-known glass painter, and some of his own work can be seen, for example, in the windows of the chapel of Queen's College, Oxford. The glass here has been subject to later alterations, as the presence of some nineteenth century panels indicates. A detailed inventory is not possible; the following are the most interesting points. The glass in the heads of the main lights, if not in situ, probably comes from the chancel side windows, and consists of canopy work of c.1320 - 40. The window contains much heraldry of various periods up to the eighteenth century (much of the glass painting of the seventeenth and eighteenth centuries was heraldic), and the earliest is probably the third shield up in the first light. A list in the chancel gives details of the families involved. The two other main types of fragments worthy of close attention are the numerous heads, mainly of the sixteenth century, and the English fifteenth century roundels, which are of special interest. They are of both sacred and secular subjects, and are delightful specimens of miniature glass painting, and worth listing: light 2 - two birds playing trumpet and harp; light 3 - St. Christopher and *Scs Johannes* and eagle, St. John's symbol; light 5 - the Virgin Mary from a Coronation, and St. Edmund. Note also in the centre south chancel window a slightly later roundel of a man killing an ox (one of the Labours of the Months).

Hardwick

This is not the most exciting display of medieval glass in Norfolk, but many churches contain such collections of fragments as we see here, and it is worth considering how to approach them. One of the first things to look for is any glass which appears to be in situ. We can be sure of nothing here, but the blue roundel with four radiating green leaves and a red border in the north east chancel window may well be in its original position (compare the roundels at **Merton**). Unfortunately, at the time of writing, it suffers from the growth of algae, a common source of the disfigurement of old glass. Notice also in this opening a piece of early sixteenth century glass, possibly part of two initials joined by a 'true lovers' knot. Next, we should look for any reasonably complete sections - the best here are the shield in the east window with the arms of Shelton impaling Morley, dating from c. 1500, and another shield of arms in the north west chancel window, with only the Shelton coat surviving in the sinister impalement. Apart from this, it is a question of looking at a few of the larger fragments - note the two fourteenth century patterned quarries in the two eastern windows, and some finely detailed pieces of fourteenth century canopy work in the south west window.

Shelton

The building of this beautiful brick church must have been started before 1497, for in that year Sir Ralph Shelton ordered in his will that it should be finished as it was begun. Much of the original glazing survives, and seems to have been carried out a few years later, for a will of 1504 leaves money for some of the glass, but it has been the subject of much later rearrangement, when both earlier and later glass has been inserted. The early sixteenth century glass is mainly secular, with many small donor figures, too numerous to itemize, but interesting examples of late gothic English glass painting with incipient renaissance details in the canopy work and settings. There are also many shields, part of a long series of Shelton family connections originally in the side windows, the lower range of which retains an unusual but monotonous series of the Shelton rebus — a shell on a tun, or barrel, with faded mottoes above. The fragmentary Resurrection scene and large standing female figure (with male tonsured head!) in the north aisle east window are examples of early sixteenth century glass painting done in England by, or under the strong influence of, North European glass painters. The highest quality painting is found in the two donor figures in the east window of the other aisle, but here the painting is so Germanic that one is tempted to conclude that these are in fact foreign panels imported at a later stage. A strong additional reason for doubting that they are part of the original glazing is the fact that the shields of arms which now make them appear as John Shelton and his wife Anne Boleyn (not the famous Anne!), do not belong to the panels, and are insertions of earlier glass. This is confirmed by the crests, which are original, and have no relation to the Sheltons or Boleyns. Finally, it should perhaps be noted that the figures in the main east window of the Virgin Mary and two Kings are mainly nineteenth century glass.

Plate X Shelton

Tour 6

Kimberley

The English glass in the east window varies in date from the early to the late fourteenth century. The earliest is in the tracery where there is a head of Christ, with sun and moon (drawn with faces) on either side. The two main openings have a seated Christ displaying his wounds, and a Crucifixion. A figure of a bishop and St. James in clearer glass may be slightly earlier in date than the series of apostles and musical angels from tracery lights, and the larger figure of St. Margaret (see **Mileham**) standing in a canopy niche, which all appear to be from the last quarter of the fourteenth century. This last figure is especially noteworthy and beautiful. The figure is elegant, though now much corroded, and the architectural setting has the careful draughtsmanship and attention to spatial effects characteristic of the period. Note however how the essentially two-dimensional feeling of English glass painting is maintained by the contrasting flatness of the diapered background. Part of a similar canopy setting now frames a sadly broken figure in early sixteenth century German glass of a weeping woman. The two large angels in this window, and the pair with scrolls in the south chancel window are of similar date and origin and are spare panels from the glass given to **Hingham** in the early nineteenth century. Two other panels in this window show Christ expelling the money lenders from the Temple and a later scene of the General Resurrection. They are both part of the Steinfeld Glazing (see Introduction, and **Erpingham**), from window 11, c. 1530 - 1 and window 24, 1555, respectively.

Plate XI Kimberley

Hingham

This is the most impressive display of imported foreign glass in a county rich in this field, but less is known about it at the moment than about other such collections we have seen. All the glass in the east window is German early sixteenth century work, apart from a certain amount of nineteenth century glass painted to fill the gaps when the panels were inserted into the specially re-made stonework in 1825. The central light contains a figure of St. Anne holding the Madonna with the Holy Child in her arms; above, stands the figure of St. Thomas with T-square, and a book in a pouch. The six side lights have four main scenes: on the north side, the Crucifixion above,

and the Deposition below, and on the north side, the Ascension over the Resurrection.
In the background of the Deposition is a small scene of the Entombment, and the
Resurrection also has depictions of the Harrowing of Hell, and Christ's Appearances to the Three
Marys and to St. Thomas, and St. Peter. Above the Christ of the Resurrection are two angels
bearing scrolls with *Resurrexit sicut dixit alleluia,* which remind us of the two similar figures at
Kimberley. Lord Woodhouse of Kimberley gave the glass here and to his own village church.
The Ascension scene includes the Heavenly Host surrounding the ascending Christ, amongst
whom we recognize Adam and Eve, Moses and David, and Melchizedek. In the tracery, the central
figure is of a male saint carrying a staff and an open book; to the right is a kneeling man in armour;
the one on the left is a copy. On either side is an angel holding the mantling of a now lost
heraldic achievement, again as at Kimberley. The style of this glass points to a Rhenish, probably
Cologne origin. The Deposition scene is painted from the same design as one at Schleiden in the Eifel
region of Germany, not far from Cologne.

Old Buckenham

Heraldry plays an important part in the study of stained glass. Not only did the medieval and
later glass painters produce some of the finest examples of heraldic art, but the historical
evidence provided by the coats of arms is often vital for dating the windows. In many churches,
the heraldry has disappeared, but the old antiquarians were avid collectors of blazons and often
recorded the now missing shields of arms. Here we have both the records and the glass. Slight
changes have been made since the last published description; the shields as they now stand
represent: Easternmost south aisle window - 1. St. George. 2. Cailly quartering Clifton. 3. Thorp.
4. A combination of two shields - Thorp impaling ---, and (probably) the same as 2. 5. Knyvet
(new). 6. Bokenham. Next window - 7. East Anglia. 8. Cromwell quartering Tatershall.
9. Knyvet quartering Clifton. 10. as 2. 11. as 9. 12. Buckenham Priory. North chancel window -
13. Kerdeston quartering quarterly --- and Bosville. Both the aisle windows have the same basic
design, with angels holding shields in the main register of the tracery lights, saints above, and
angels bearing scrolls in the heads of the main lights, but they differ in detail, both between each
other, and internally, the tracery light angels being clearly different from those below in each
case. The scrolls bear (restored) texts in praise of the Virgin Mary, taken from various church
offices, and similar to those once found in the Lady Chapel of St. Stephen's Norwich, where the
main subject of the window was the Life of the Virgin Mary. That window was made in 1461,
and the glass here probably dates c. 1460 - 80. Further study of the heraldry, which relates
to local land owners and their family connections, will perhaps make the dating more precise.
The saints in the tracery are fairly uncommon - St. Botulph and St. Leonard (with chain) in
the eastern window, and St. Peter Martyr (a monk holding a sword, with a dagger in his side) in
the other.

East Harling

The glass in the main lights of the east window is practically all of fifteenth century date and owes
its preservation to the fact that it was removed and stored at the hall at a time when it would other-
wise almost certainly have been destroyed by religious iconoclasm or neglect. The bottom left
and right panels show the first two of the three husbands of Anne Harling, a rich heiress largely
responsible for the rebuilding and glazing of the church. On the right is Sir William Chamberlain,
who died in 1462, and on the left, Sir Robert Wingfield, who died in 1480. Beneath the latter is
a request for prayers the wording of which implies that he was still alive when the glass was made.
Additional documentary evidence narrows the date range to 1463 - 80. Although no definite
evidence connects these panels to those above, it is very probable that the main part of the
glazing, consisting of fifteen scenes from the Life of the Virgin Mary, is contemporary with them.
The scenes are as follows: the Annunciation; the Visitation; the Nativity (note the two midwives);
the Adoration of the Shepherds; the Adoration of the Magi; the Presentation in the Temple;
Christ among the Doctors; the Wedding at Cana; the Betrayal; the Crucifixion; the Pieta; the

Plate XII East Harling

Resurrection; the Ascension; Pentecost (these last two based on reversed cartoons); and finally the Assumption of the Virgin Mary. Other more fragmentary panels include a figure of Mary Magdalene, one with angels holding texts from the Te Deum, and another with the head of St. Gregory, and parts of a lost figure of Anne Harling, still to be seen in the east window in the eighteenth century. The Life of the Virgin series here has been said to be by the same artists as did the Mancroft series. However, although some of the same design sources are used, and the style of the painting is clearly connected with that at Mancroft, particularly with the Life of St. Peter series, here it is a later version, coarser, more vigorous, and with more angular drapery folds.

The Mancroft Life of Christ panels are larger and more detailed compositions, but the Harling scenes often give the impression of being more crowded. The Crucifixion, for instance, has fitted into a very small area many characters who usually only appear in larger compositions. Lesser remains in other windows include interesting heraldic badges, and rather repetitive demi-figures of angels, all of similar date.

Merton

The glass in this church is of several different periods and all worthy of attention, apart from the rather inferior Victorian glass in the east window and the main lights of the north nave windows. Although the chancel side windows appear to date from c. 1300, what looks like parts of their original glazing is rather later, c. 1320 - 30. Most of it is in the north east window, where we can see three partly restored figures (the heads are new) of saints, of which the second is clearly St. Margaret and the third now represents St. John, but may originally have been St. Catherine. The old glass is of good quality - note the varied diaper patterns and the fine red dragon. The canopy above the figure is mostly genuine, but the pedestals come from a nineteenth century artist's imagination. The rest of the main light chancel figures are of c. 1830-40 and not very good, but are an interesting example of a new archaeological approach to restoration, being a brave but mis-conceived attempt to reproduce the style of the original glass. The tracery glass in the three windows is mostly of the fifteenth and nineteenth centuries. In the nave the following should be noted: fragments of a fifteenth century angel in the tracery of a south window; in the main lights of the south windows, pieces of the fifteenth and much of the nineteenth centuries, but also some interesting heraldic medallions, very similar to some at **Saxlingham Nethergate**, and of which the first and fourth are of the sixteenth to seventeenth centuries, and the second and third are nineteenth century copies (note the spider and fly on the sundial); in the east window of the aisle is nineteenth century heraldic glass, possibly based on a coat of arms of Tudor date.

Ashill

The figured tracery panels hung against the north nave windows represent parts of two series. They are in excellent condition apart from the loss of the original heads, which have been replaced by other medieval heads. Although many of our figures in glass are now headless as the result of an attenuated but disfiguring form of religious iconoclasm, cases are known where the heads have been removed by unscrupulous collectors. Of the two series mentioned, the more complete is that of the Four Doctors of the church seated, as at **Saxlingham Nethergate**, at writing desks. St. Augustine, St. Gregory, and St. Jerome are here, but St. Ambrose is missing. The other figures are two of the four Evangelists - St. John with the eagle at his feet, and St. Matthew with a winged man, partly lost. Both these series were common in glass and on screens, (the doors of the screens were often reserved for the Doctors). Here, the two sets are in the same style and clearly went together. The Apostles were represented in various ways - at Banningham there are the remains of a very similar set to this, but at **Stratton Strawless**, they are seated, as the Doctors are here. The rod and leaf border round these panels is very common in Norfolk glass, but also occurs in many other areas and in other media, including manuscript painting, wood carving and wall painting. Of the other pieces here, which include decorative filling with rose and seed pod motifs, the best is a fine Maria monogram which retains its original rod and leaf border. All the glass here is Norwich work of the period c. 1460-80.

Tour 7

North Tuddenham

Woodforde tells us that the medieval glass here, apart from two or three shields of arms, was not made for this church. He says that it was discarded from a Norfolk church, and suggests Lyng, or Billingford, near North Elmham, as possible sources. Two of the panels in the west window here show scenes from the life of St. Margaret, and may well have come from Lyng, which was dedicated to that saint. The rest of the glass, figures and scenes from tracery lights, placed in the other windows, could not have come from there, as it would not have fitted the tracery lights. It is at present awaiting restoration. We will confine our attentions to the glass now in the church, which consists of the above-mentioned St. Margaret panels, and one with scenes from the Life of St. George, all main light panels. The panel on the left shows St. Margaret of Antioch spinning and keeping sheep in a field. The provost Olybrius has seen her while riding by, and we see his servant asking her to come with him to his master. In the second, central scene, Olybrius is shown questioning Margaret, asking her whether she is a slave or free, to which she replies that she is not free, but a Christian. Woodforde lists other series, both extant and lost, which indicate

Plate XIII North Tuddenham

some of the scenes which would have completed this partial cycle of the life of St. Margaret. As we cannot be sure of the provenance of these panels, we must look at the internal evidence of the panels themselves for an indication of date. First there is the costume of the figures. This is striking, being of the high-necked, narrow waisted, rather fantastical type introduced into this country from France during the reign of Richard II, and which persisted well into the fifteenth century. The style of the facial and figure drawing also suggests an early fifteenth century date - elegant figures with courtly, rather supercilious expressions and fashionable pointed beards, their rather bulky garments drawn with voluminous, often convoluted folds - all contributing to a definite 'International Gothic' feeling (the name for the general European style of art in the years either side of 1400). It is true that certain features of this style linger on in Norfolk until the mid-century, but the particular combination here, I feel, cannot be other than real International Gothic. Confirmation of such date is given by the close resemblance of the canopy forms to some in **Saxlingham Nethergate** church, dateable on historical and heraldic evidence probably to c. 1390 - 1413 but which look just a little earlier than the ones here. The third panel here shows two scenes from the Life of St. George - the Saint speaking with the king's daughter, and his attack on the dragon. The style is rather different, but it is probably of a similar date to the St. Margaret panels.

Mileham

The west window gives us the best impression we can have in Norfolk of what a typical complete fourteenth century window would have looked like - in the main lights, large single figures of saints surrounded by tall elaborate canopies, and beneath, a horizontal band of quarry glazing relieved by roundels containing heraldry, (cf. **Elsing**), grotesques (cf. **Ringland**), or as here, sacred monograms. The emphasis of the design is on strong vertical and horizontal accents, and the colouring of the period, although richer than much fifteenth century work, stresses the inter-mediate tones of yellow, brown and green, without the predominance of primary colours characteristic of thirteenth century and fifteenth century glazing. Note how, unlike the fifteenth century the fourteenth century curvilinear tracery forms leave little room for figured glazing, and decorative foliage patterns are often, as here, used instead. Where figure-work does appear in the tracery of fourteenth century windows, as at **Great Walsingham**, it often betrays the difficulty of adapting it to the unusual forms. The three main figures here are St. Catherine, St. John the Baptist, and St. Margaret. This latter figure is based on the same design as the later figure at **Kimberley**. There are also smaller figures from other windows - another fourteenth century St. John the Baptist (the church bears his name), and two fifteenth century figures of St. Barbara and St. Margaret. The east window has a fourteenth century figure of St. John? the Evangelist and a bishop, and a fifteenth century St. Agatha, and a south chancel window has a curious fifteenth century panel showing two pack horses followed by a man and a woman and *Broun* in lettering.

Litcham

Here again are the remains of what must have been high quality glazing. They are set in a north window and repay close attention. First, notice the tiny angels in the twin eyelets over the first and third main lights. Figure work in such small openings is comparatively unusual in the fifteenth century and indicates a rich and detailed arrangement. They also here possibly formed an interesting psychological link between the subject matter of the larger tracery lights and the main lights below, for three of the angels look downwards and one looks up. The twin main tracery openings and the presence of angels suggest that the tracery may have held a Coronation of the Virgin (as at **South Acre** and **Ketteringham**, for example); below this may have been represented the previous and penultimate scene in the story of the Virgin Mary, her Assumption. The two other smaller openings contain nineteenth century decorative filling, but the larger ones above have an arrangement of interesting fragments, probably from the main lights below. They mostly consist of parts of what must have been a sumptuous canopy whose side shafting was inhabited by figures of lions and men. The use of lions in canopy work is quite common in Norfolk, but the presence of small male figures (often said to be prophets) is unusual in East Anglia. There is part of one in later glass in St. Peter Mancroft and others in glass of a more similar date at Cawston. The delicacy of drawing, the forked beard and elegant pose of the top figure suggest a date in the first quarter of the fifteenth century and the glass is probably to be associated with the re-dedication of the church which took place in 1412.

Tour 7

West Rudham

In 1972 the author visited this church and found this beautiful glass in a dreadful condition - so dirty that a true appreciation of its quality was hardly possible. At the time of writing, two panels have been cleaned and releaded, revealing highly interesting fine glass painting, surprisingly little affected by the layers of dirt. The glass should be replaced some time in 1975. It consists of the following: westernmost window on the north side of the nave - a six winged feathered angel and a figure of Christ displaying his wounds, in the tracery, and a canopy top in the head of one main light. Centre north nave window — tracery, top centre, a seated figure of Christ wearing a crown of thorns; beneath, a Coronation of the Virgin, flanked on the right by a figure of Gabriel from an Annunciation. Eastern north nave window — tracery, top centre, the remains of a lily pot; tracery light below, far left, St. Mark with a lion. The heads of the outer main lights have canopy tops. This disposition of subjects is difficult to understand; it would make more sense, for instance, if the lily pot and the Annunciation were in the same window. There is no historical or heraldic evidence to help us with the donors or dating of this glass; the style, however, is very interesting. To be more accurate, it should be styles, for there are two distinct types of painting here. Both occur together in the central window, thus indicating that they are contemporaneous; they are best seen (at least until the Gabriel figure is cleaned) in the figure of the Virgin Mary from the Coronation and in that of Christ displaying His wounds. The first is characterised by a sweetness of expression, with large forehead, small chin and soft round eyes, and also by the bulkiness of its drapery forms. The second, by its refinement, with carefully drawn features, drapery which falls in soft controlled curves and a dignified and restrained, if rather courtly, pose. The difference is marked and points to a period of transition. The first style is the earlier and

Plate XIV West Rudham

reminds one in general terms of the art of the early fifteenth century and, more particularly, of the work of the illuminator, Herman Scheere. The second style is unusual for its high quality; the nearest parallel is with the earliest work in St. Peter Mancroft, Norwich, the Infancy cycle of c. 1440, with which it shares the elegance of pose and the refined linear facial drawing. This combination of the old and the new in style would make a date in the period 1430-40 the most likely for this glass.

Harpley

Here binoculars are essential! The tracery of the lofty fifteenth century west window has a dozen figures of saints, an Annunciation, a donor figure and fragments of canopy work and quarry glazing. The central feature is the Annunciation, below which are seated figures of the English royal saints, Edmund and Edward the Confessor (based on cartoons of the Coronation of the Virgin) and flanked by standing figures of St. James, the Great (very like that at Rougham) and St. John, the Evangelist. The outer arch of the tracery has a series of ecclesiastical saints and a male donor at the top, with the invocation *ora pro nobis*. The saints on the left in ascending order are: St. Wilfred, Archbishop; a saint in deacon's vestment, possibly St. Lawrence, as the church bears his name, and two other deacon saints are present, including the next saint, St. Vincent; St. Ledger, bishop. On the right, in descending order: St. Thomas of Canterbury, archbishop; St. Martin, bishop; St. Stephen, deacon; St. Blaise, bishop. Parts of a few figures are restored. This is an interesting iconographical scheme, showing an individual choice of saints, as at Wiggenhall St. Mary Magdalene, where the rather ugly facial style of these figures can be paralleled. In the small openings below the transom, are a series of the Orders of Angels, as at Oxburgh. The east window of the south aisle contains very restored canopies of the first half of the fourteenth century.

Great Massingham

The glass here is a good example of one of the very common cheaper types of fifteenth century work, showing many of the characteristic features of the glass of the region. One has to be very careful when talking about regional peculiarities in glass-painting, for it is easy to overlook the fact that a detail which recurs may be not just a local, but a national feature. However, several decorative traits of the glass here are met so often in this county that when they occur in combination, as here, we are safe in assuming a definite 'Norwich' style, although it must not be forgotten that the painting of the heads and, to a lesser extent, the drapery, is an equally important determining aspect of the style. First, let us examine the subject matter. The chancel has only three side windows (there does not appear to have been a fourth) and the tracery of each has four main openings - an ideal opportunity for a series of Twelve Apostles, which is, in fact, the subject of the remaining figures. The easternmost south window retains those of St. Peter, an unidentified figure, St. James the Less, St. Bartholomew. The next window has an Apostle with a halberd, St. Matthias, St. Simon, St. Jude and one with a tau cross, St. Matthew. The head of the central main light contains a canopy top, the top tracery light the Agnus Dei, and lesser openings have 'pod' decoration, as do those of the window opposite, whose only other surviving glass is a head of Christ in the top quatrefoil. The Apostles, all of whom, except the last, have lost their heads, stand on pedestals decorated with the 'ears of barley' pattern, against folded screens with 'seaweed' pattern, and are surmounted by a wavy star in the top foil, all characteristic devices of this region. The style of the head in the north window shows the strong, linear facial drawing, typical of Norwich work, best seen in the St. Peter series in St. Peter Mancroft.

South Acre

Fragments of three different dates can be seen here. The east window of the north aisle contains remains of late thirteenth century grisaille glazing - the most complete example in the county.

Much of this type of cheaper, non-figurative glass-painting must have been seen in our parish churches in the middle ages, particularly before the extensive rebuilding which occurred in the next two centuries. Here the white glass is decorated with naturalistic leaf rinceaux and relieved with touches of blue, yellow and red. The adjacent north window contains equally interesting remains. Blomefield tells us that Sir John Harsyk rebuilt the north aisle and ordered in his will, proved in 1383, that he be buried in the chapel of the Assumption, which was at the east end of the north aisle, in a window of which were his wife's and his own portraits. Very probably, this window also had a representation of the Assumption of the Virgin Mary, over which was the scene of her Coronation, still to be seen in fragmentary state in the tracery. The interesting canopy tops below indicate that a date around the time of Sir John's death would suit this glass - they have the rounded, three-dimensional forms characteristic of the period. The westernmost south nave window has a medley of fifteenth century pieces, mainly eyelet-filling decorated with the rose-en-soleil.

Glossary

Abrasion	All red or ruby and certain blue and other coloured glass was made from a double layer of coloured and white glass. The coloured layer was sometimes abraded or scraped away with a flint to reveal the white beneath, and thus allow two colours on the same piece of glass. Most often used in heraldry and patterned garments.
Canopy	Architectural setting for a figure or scene. Usually had side-shafts and a pedestal, but often only the top survives.
Cartoon	Full scale design for the window painted at first on whitened boards and later on paper or parchment rolls. Often used or adapted for several different panels.
Creed Scroll	A common subject in late medieval art was a set of the Twelve Apostles each carrying a scroll bearing a portion of the Creed.
Donor Figures	Kneeling figures in the glass of the people who gave the glass, or of their friends, relations and colleagues.
Ears of Barley Pattern	A decorative device, probably meant to represent the grain of wood, and very common in fifteenth century local work in Norfolk.
Grisaille	Here, non-figurative glass with an overall decorative pattern, based on geometrical and leaf forms and mainly using clear glass. Not, however, usually applied to glazing using patterned quarries (q.v.).
Iconography	The way in which subject matter is portrayed.
Main Light	A single area of glass bounded by the stonework of a window between the tracery and the bottom of the window.
Messianic Texts	The Old Testament parallel to Creed Scrolls (q.v.), was a set of Twelve of the Prophets carrying texts from the Old Testament which were thought to have foretold the coming of the Messiah.
Orders of Angels	In medieval art, the different types of angels mentioned in the Bible were gathered together into a hierarchy consisting of Nine Orders. The Nine Orders were sometimes distinguished by labels, as at Salle, but often just by attributes, which, however, varied considerably.
Patterned Quarries	Diamond shaped pieces of glass decorated with mainly floral and leaf patterns, used for the simplest and cheapest type of glazing.
Rebus	A visual pun on a person's name, e.g. a shell on a tun (barrel), for Shelton.
Rose-en-Soleil	A white rose set on a yellow rayed sun. The badge of Edward the Fourth, and a common device for patterned quarries (q.v.).
Seaweed Diaper	A diaper is an overall decorative pattern on a background or on drapery. A distinctive type resembling seaweed, but really deriving from a leaf pattern, is common in fifteenth century local work in Norfolk.
Smear and Stipple Shading	The two main methods of modelling drapery, faces, etc. in medieval glass painting. Smear shading is a thin solution of brown paint applied with parallel brush strokes. Stipple shading is a wash of paint which has been stippled with the end of the brush, giving greater translucence. It was introduced in the late fourteenth century and largely replaced smear shading.
Stained Glass	An accepted mis-nomer. Painted glass is normally more correct, as the only stain used is silver or yellow stain for the yellow details

of hair, costume, etc. It was first used in the early fourteenth century in this country. The other colours (except in later enamelled glass) are in the glass itself and not applied. The actual painting is done in a brown or grey pigment used for the drawing and modelling of hands, faces, drapery, etc.

Tracery Light   A single area of glass bounded by an opening in the tracery of a window. The very small apertures are normally known as 'eyelets'.

Select Bibliography

There is not room in this small book for the full critical apparatus of references and footnotes, nor for an extensive bibliography. What follows is a brief indication of the main sources for those who wish to proceed further with the study of stained glass in Norfolk.

General Books on English Stained Glass

Of the many such works, the most useful are:
WINSTON, C., **An Inquiry into the Differences of Style Observable in Ancient Glass Paintings, Especially in England.** London, 1847.
WESTLAKE, N.H.J., **History of Design in Painted Glass,** 4 vols. London, 1879-94.
NELSON, P., **Ancient Painted Glass in England.** London, 1913.
LE COUTEUR, J.D., **English Mediaeval Painted Glass.** London, 1926.
READ, H., **English Stained Glass.** London, 1926.
WOODFORDE, C., **English Stained and Painted Glass.** Oxford, 1954.
READ, H., BAKER, J., LAMMER, A., **English Stained Glass.** London, 1960.

Norfolk Stained Glass

For the antiquarian background to the history of the glass, there are three main sources:
BLOMEFIELD, F., and PARKIN, C., **An Essay towards a Topographical History of the County of Norfolk,** 11 vols. London, 1805-10, and the manuscript collections of Thomas Martin and Anthony Norris (both of the eighteenth century), in the Norfolk Record Office, Rye MSS 17 and 6 respectively. For the region as a whole, see: WOODFORDE, C., **The Norwich School of Glass Painting in the Fifteenth Century.** London, 1950. This largely superseded a number of earlier articles and books by the same author and others; these are not listed here. The Exhibition Catalogue, **Medieval Art in East Anglia 1300 - 1520.** Norwich, 1973, ed. LASKO, P., and MORGAN, N.J., has several entries on individual panels of local glass, and a number of general essays. There are many articles and a few books which deal with the glass in individual churches. The following are the most important:
ACOMB, H.W., 'The Flemish Glass at Earsham', in, **A Supplement to Blomefield's History of Norfolk,** ed. INGLEBY, C. London, 1929. pp. 71-80.
HARFORD, D., 'On the East Window of St. Stephen's Church, Norwich', in, **Norfolk Archaeology** (hereafter **N.A.**'), vol. xv. pp. 335-348.
HUNTER, J., 'The History and Topography of Ketteringham, in the County of Norfolk', in, **N.A.**, vol. iii. pp. 245-314.
INGLEBY, C., 'Denton and its Glass', in, **A Supplement to Blomefield's History of Norfolk,** ed. INGLEBY, C. London, 1929. 47-69.
KENT, E.A., 'Stained and Painted Glass in the Guildhall, Norwich', in, **N.A.,** vol. xxiii. pp. 1-10.
---- 'Some Heraldic Glass in Norwich', in, **Journal of the British Society of Master Glass Painters** (hereafter '**J.B.S.M.G.P.**'), vol. iv. pp. 137-141.
KEYSER, C.E., 'Notes on Some Fifteenth-Century Glass in the Church of Wiggenhall St. Mary Magdalene', in, **N.A.,** vol. xvi. pp. 306-319.
---- 'Notes on Some Ancient Stained Glass in Sandringham Church, Norfolk', in, **N.A.,** vol. xix. pp. 122-132.
KING, D.G., 'The Releading and Rearrangement of Ancient Glass in Bale Church', in, **J.B.S.M.G.P.,** vol. viii. pp. 58-62.
KING, G.A., 'On the Ancient Stained Glass Still Remaining in the Church of St. Peter Hungate, Norwich', in, **N.A.,** vol. xvi. pp. 205-218.
---- 'The Pre-Reformation Painted Glass in St. Andrew's Church, Norwich', in, **N.A.,** vol. xviii. pp. 283-294.
PARSONS, W.L.E., **Salle.** Norwich, 1937.
SINGH, Prince F.D., 'Armorial Glass in Old and New Buckenham Churches', in, **N.A.,** vol. xv. pp. 324-334.